Amazing Athletes

40 inspiring icons

Jean-Michel Billioud & Gonoh

WIDE EYED EDITIONS

Wonder, question, discover

Ever since the French baron Pierre de Coubertin had the good idea to relaunch the Olympic Games in 1896 and the Paralympic Games was started in 1960, thousands of champions have thrilled crowds around the world with their sporting exploits. In this book you will meet forty of the most magnificent athletes from throughout history. Some athletes have become legendary after a single feat. The Greek athlete Spyridon Louis, for example, was the first winner of the marathon in 1896 and the American Bob Beamon broke the record for the long jump of 55cm in 1968.

But most of the athletes in this book stand out becuase of their significance in a particular sport over a period of time. Between them, they have amassed a huge number of medals and broken numerous world records. You may have heard of Mo Farah, Simone Biles, Usain Bolt, Michael Phelps, and Ellie Simmonds. But do you know about the epic Fanny Blankers-Koen, the only woman to have won four gold medals in a single olympiad (100m, 200m, 4x100m, and 80m hurdles)?

Some of these legends have not only made history in the pool, on the track, or on the apparatus. In 1936, Jesse Owens dared to challenge Hitler; in 1968, Tommie Smith stepped onto the podium, wearing a black glove with his fist raised to protest against racial segregation in the United States. In 2000, the First Nations athlete Cathy Freeman, symbolized the resumed dialogue between First Nations people and the Australian state.

Whatever their history and their performance, each of these 40 champions deserve their place at the top of the poduim. Get your sneakers on and prepare to meet 40 amazing athletes.

Contents

1
SPYRIDON LOUIS

2
CHARLOTTE
COOPER

3
MADGE SYERS

4
JIM THORPE

5
PAAVO NURMI

6
MILDRED "BABE"
DIDRIKSON ZAHARIAS

7
JESSE OWENS

8
FANNY
BLANKERS-KOEN

9
EMIL ZÁTOPEK

10
MARJORIE GESTRING

11
MICHELINE
OSTERMEYER

12
ABEBE BIKILA

13
BETTY CUTHBERT

14
WILMA RUDOLPH

15
TOMMIE SMITH

16
MARK SPITZ

17
DALEY THOMPSON

18
CARL LEWIS

19
NADIA COMĂNECI

20
BIRGIT FISCHER

21 STEVE REDGRAVE

22 NAWAL EL MOUTAWAKEL

23 TRISCHA ZORN

24 JONAS JACOBSSON

25 SEBASTIAN COE

26 MICHAEL JOHNSON

27 MARIE-JOSÉ PÉREC

28 MICHAEL EDGSON

29 ISABELL WERTH

30 MARIA MUTOLA

31 CATHY FREEMAN

32 VALENTINA VEZZALI

33 TONY ESTANGUET

34 YELENA ISINBAYEVA

35 MO FARAH

36 MICHAEL PHELPS

37 USAIN BOLT

38 TEDDY RINER

39 ELLIE SIMMONDS

40 SIMONE BILES

Spyridon Louis

BIOGRAPHY

Jan 1873–
Mar 1940

Greek

Athletics

Marathon

Main rival:
Charilaos Vasilakos
(Greek)

This runner, who earned his living as a water carrier, made his name by winning the marathon at the first modern-day Summer Olympics, held in Athens in 1896, when he was 23 years old. Although he wasn't the favorite to win, he took the lead with 2.5 miles to go and won the race (which was 24.85 miles that year) by more than 7 minutes. There were even rumors that he was so confident that he took a break to have a glass of wine at the midway point. Crown Prince Constantine and his brother Prince George of Greece ran the final lap of the track with him. A million spectators went wild, as all three athletes on the podium were Greek.

UNLIKELY PRIZES

Spyridon Louis's prizes included a trophy, but also an antique vase, a donkey cart, and a barber's voucher that entitled him to free shaves for life!

BELATED RECOGNITION

Forty years after his victory, Spyridon Louis was the flagbearer for the Greek team at the 1936 Olympics in Berlin.

AFTERWARDS

He became a farmer, then a police officer.

"That moment was incredible, and I still remember it like a vivid dream."

HATLESS

Unlike the others in the race, he ran without a cap in the intense heat.

MEDALS

1896

SNEAKERS

His running shoes were a gift from the people of his village.

FASHION

He wore three-quarter-length shorts with a belt.

RECORD
He completed the 24.85 miles in 2 hours 58 minutes 50 seconds.

The national hero

Charlotte Cooper

BIOGRAPHY

Sep 1870–
Oct 1966

British

Tennis

Main rival:
Hélène Prévost
(French)

Known for her aggressive attacking game, this English tennis player was the favorite at the 1900 Olympics, having been Wimbledon champion in 1895, 1896, and 1898. No one was surprised when she won the mixed doubles and singles on the clay courts of the Ile de Puteaux, an island in the middle of the River Seine. She won every match in straight sets and became the first woman to win an Olympic singles title!

WHERE ARE THE WOMEN?

Women didn't take part in the 1896 Olympics, but in 1900, they competed in shooting, sailing, horse riding, golf, and tennis, as well as croquet and fishing.

11

Charlotte Cooper reached 11 Wimbledon finals between 1895 and 1912!

1900 OLYMPICS

The Games took place between mid-May and the end of October 1900, as part of the World's Fair.

UNBEATABLE

Charlotte Cooper won Wimbledon again in 1901 and 1908. She was 37 years and 296 days old when she won her last title. No one has ever equaled this record.

MEDALS

1900

POWER PLAY

At the time, Charlotte Cooper was one of the few players who threw the ball up above her head to serve.

GUTSTY GEAR

She used a wooden racket with strings that would have been made from cow or sheep gut.

STYLE OF THE TIMES

Like all female players, she competed in a long dress.

RECORD
She won Wimbledon 5 times.

Queen of the courts

Madge Syers

BIOGRAPHY

Sep 1881–
Sep 1917

British

Figure skating

Main rival:
Elsa Rendschmidt
(German)

World figure-skating champion in 1906 and 1907, Madge Syers blew away the crowds and judges with her precision and technical skill. At the London Games in 1908, she won the Olympic title in the ladies' competition and the bronze medal in the pairs event with her husband and trainer, Edgar. The young Englishwoman is the only female skater to win pairs and individual medals at the same Olympics. She retired shortly after the London Games because of poor health and wrote books about the art of figure skating.

TENACIOUS

Madge Syers participated in the men's category in the world championships in 1902 because there was no category for women. She finished second in the competition, smashing everyone's expectations.

1900 OLYMPICS

They took place over almost 6 months, with 2,008 athletes competing from 22 countries. Only 2% were women.

AFTERWARDS

Madge Syers sadly died of a heart attack in 1917, at just 35 years old.

ICE IN SUMMER

The last time skating was featured in the Summer Olympic Games was 1920. In 1924, it became part of the first Winter Olympic Games held in Chamonix.

RECORD
She won the first two Women's Figure Skating World Championships in 1906 and 1907 and came second in the Mixed World Championships in 1902.

ELEGANCE
She always topped off her outfit with a stylish hat.

MEDALS
1908

NEVER WITHOUT...
... her ice skates

PERFECTIONIST
She was the first to perform technically perfect jumps.

The ice fairy

Jim Thorpe

BIOGRAPHY

May 1888–
Mar 1953

American

Athletics

Pentathlon
and decathlon

Main rival:
Hugo Wieslander
(Swedish)

This all-around sportsman was from the Sac and Fox and Potawatomi tribes and grew up in Oklahoma. He won the pentathlon (long jump, javelin, discus, 200m, and 1500m) and decathlon (100m, long jump, shot put, high jump, 400m, discus, 110m hurdles, pole vault, javelin, and 1500m) at the Stockholm Olympics in 1912. The hero of the competition, he beat the world records in both events. But his celebrations were short-lived. He was stripped of his two Olympic titles when he was accused of breaking the amateur athlete rules by being paid as a professional. They were only given back to him in 1983, 30 years after he died.

STAR OF THE BIG SCREEN

After his athletics career was over, Jim Thorpe became a film actor, playing secondary Native American roles in about 50 films.

AFTERWARDS

The town of Mauch Chunk in Pennsylvania was renamed Jim Thorpe in his honor, after it made an agreement with his widow to pay for a memorial and grave for the champion athlete.

GIFTED ALL-AROUNDER

An exceptional athlete, he was also good at baseball, had a career as a basketball player, and became one of the first big stars in professional football.

> **"Sir, you are the best athlete in the world."**
>
> Gustav V (king of Sweden) to Jim Thorpe, when he presented him with his gold medals

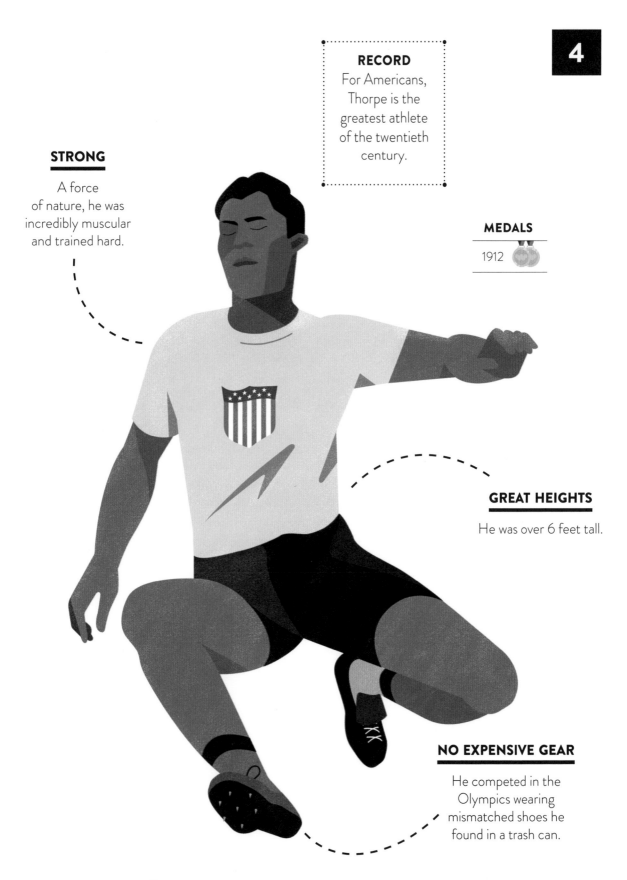

RECORD
For Americans, Thorpe is the greatest athlete of the twentieth century.

STRONG
A force of nature, he was incredibly muscular and trained hard.

MEDALS
1912

GREAT HEIGHTS
He was over 6 feet tall.

NO EXPENSIVE GEAR
He competed in the Olympics wearing mismatched shoes he found in a trash can.

The all-around athlete

Paavo Nurmi

BIOGRAPHY

Jun 1897–
Oct 1973

Finnish

Athletics

3000m, 1500m,
and 500m

Main rival:
Ville Ritola
(Finnish)

Four years after his Olympic debut in Antwerp in 1920, Finnish athlete Paavo Nurmi made history at the Paris Games, becoming the first athlete ever to win five gold medals at a single Olympics. Over four days, he won the 1500m, the 500m, the 3000m team event, and the two cross-country events. Until 1932, Paavo Nurmi was the king of long and middle-distance running, winning many Olympic medals and setting world records.

INDESTRUCTIBLE

He was suspended a few days before the Los Angeles Olympics in 1932 for being a professional, paid athlete. Still fighting at 35, he dreamed of winning the marathon.

22

The number of world records Nurmi set, over distances ranging from 1500m to 20km.

1924 OLYMPICS

There were also artistic competitions at the Games in Paris, with medals awarded in literature, architecture, and sculpture!

A GREAT HONOR

At the opening ceremony of the Helsinki Games in 1952, Paavo Nurmi had the honor of lighting the Olympic cauldron with a torch carried from Olympia in Greece, the home of the games.

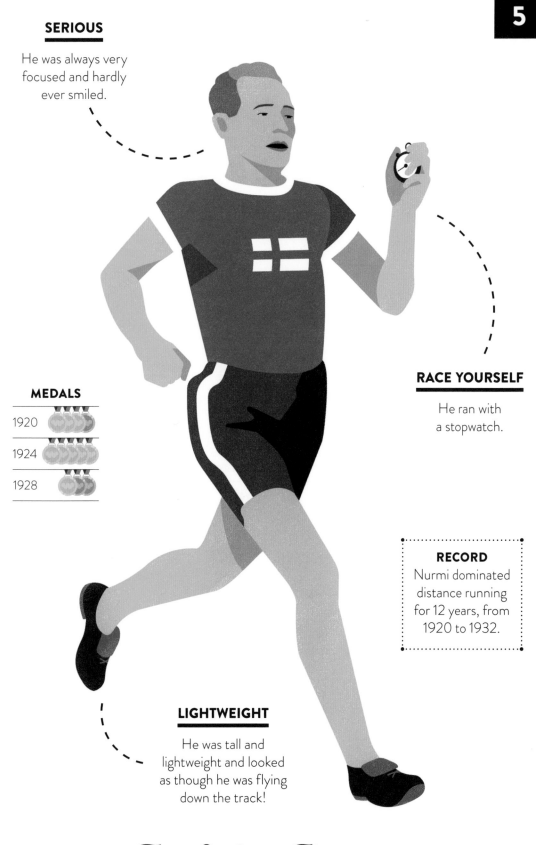

SERIOUS

He was always very focused and hardly ever smiled.

RACE YOURSELF

He ran with a stopwatch.

MEDALS

1920

1924

1928

RECORD

Nurmi dominated distance running for 12 years, from 1920 to 1932.

LIGHTWEIGHT

He was tall and lightweight and looked as though he was flying down the track!

The flying Finn

Mildred "Babe" Didrikson Zaharias

BIOGRAPHY

Jun 1911– Sep 1956

American

Athletics

Javelin, 80m hurdles, high jump, golf

Main rival: Jean Shiley (American)

The first female athletics star of the Olympics, this young American won two golds and two silvers in Los Angeles, in very different events including javelin, hurdles, and high jump! She was incredibly talented at all kinds of sports, from basketball and football to baseball. She was also a gifted skier and tennis player, and for a few years, she was even the best golfer in the world.

MULTITALENTED

Considered the best all-around female athlete in history, Mildred Didrikson was born to compete in the pentathlon, but women weren't allowed to enter that event at the Olympics until 1964.

1,000

In golf training, Mildred Didrikson used to hit 1,000 balls every day!

AFTERWARDS

As a professional golfer, she won 31 major competitions between 1948 and 1956 and became the best-paid female golfer in the world.

IMPRESSIVE

At the American qualifiers in 1952, she set four world records in a single afternoon: javelin, 80m hurdles, high jump, and baseball throw.

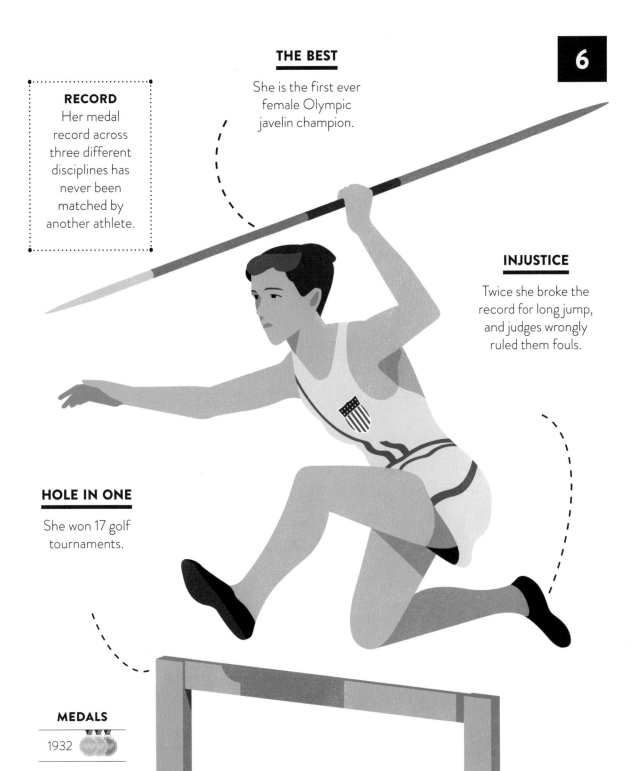

THE BEST
She is the first ever female Olympic javelin champion.

RECORD
Her medal record across three different disciplines has never been matched by another athlete.

INJUSTICE
Twice she broke the record for long jump, and judges wrongly ruled them fouls.

HOLE IN ONE
She won 17 golf tournaments.

MEDALS
1932

Gifted all-arounder

Jesse Owens

BIOGRAPHY

Sep 1913–
Mar 1980

American

Athletics

100m, 200m,
4x100m

Main rival: Luz
Long (German)

Grandson of an Alabaman slave, Jesse Owens was the undisputed hero of the Berlin Olympics in 1936. At only 22, he won four gold medals, in the 100m, 200m, 4x100m relay, and long jump. He was the first black athlete to achieve international success, and as Hitler watched on angrily from the stands, his victories proved the Nazi regime's racist ideas wrong.

ANOTHER BATTLE

After retiring from athletics, the quadruple Olympic champion used his fame to fight for civil rights denied to black people in the United States, which was still racially segregated.

AFTERWARDS

After the Olympics, Jesse became a playground instructor for underprivileged youth in Cleveland. Then he part-owned a dry cleaning business.

6

On May 25, 1935, he beat or equaled six world records in less than an hour.

PAYING HOMAGE

There is a street and a school named after him in Berlin, and two stamps were issued in his honor in the United States. A film about his victory, *Race*, was released in 2016.

RECORD
His 1935 long-jump record of 8.13m was not beaten for 25 years!

MEDALS
1936

POWERFUL AND QUICK
He was 5'10" tall and weighed 165 pounds.

A GIFT
Jesse Owens ran wearing shoes provided by Adolf Dassler, the German founder of Adidas.

LEAPING
He cleared 2m in the high jump.

The legend

Fanny Blankers-Koen

BIOGRAPHY

Apr 1918–
Jan 2004

Dutch

Athletics

100m, 200m,
4x100m,
80m hurdles

Main rival:
Dorothy Manley
(British)

After making her Olympic debut in the high jump in 1936, this Dutch athlete was the hero of the London Games twelve years later. Showing incredible speed, she comfortably won the 100m, 200m, 4x100m relay, and 80m hurdles. Four events, four gold medals, and each time her sprinting sent the crowds wild. This multitalented sportswoman was named Female Athlete of the Century in 1999 by the International Association of Athletics Federations.

UNFAIR

She could have won gold in the long jump and high jump as well, as she held the world records, but female athletes were only allowed to compete in a maximum of four events.

16

She held 16 world records in eight different events!

1948 OLYMPICS

59 countries took part in the London Olympics—Germany and Japan were not invited as they were under military occupation. It was the first Olympic Games to be shown on TV.

DEFYING EXPECTATION

Journalists called her the "flying housewife" and criticized her for training when they thought she should be with her children. Fanny knew they were being ignorant and sexist, and so she did her best to ignore them.

RECORD
She participated in three games, before and after the war in 1936, 1948, and 1952.

UNUSUAL
She was one of the few mothers to become an Olympic champion.

MEDALS
1948

FAST AND LIGHT
It looked like she was flying along the track.

REACHING NEW HEIGHTS
She was the first female athlete to clear 1.7m in the high jump.

The Dutch rocket

Emil Zátopek

BIOGRAPHY

Sep 1922–
Nov 2000

Czechoslovakian

Athletics

5000m,
10,000m,
marathon

Main rival: Alain
Mimoun (French)

Legendary athlete Emil Zátopek won gold in the 10,000m and silver in the 5000m at the London Games in 1948. Four years later, in Helsinki, he won the 5000m, 10,000m, and marathon. He is the only athlete to have won all three events at the same Olympic Games. Zátopek was the first athlete to run the 10,000m in under 29 minutes, a record that remained unbeaten from 1948 until 1954.

PRODIGY

In Helsinki, although he'd never won a marathon at a competitive meet, he won with a lead of two and a half minutes, setting a new Olympic record of 2hrs 23min 3s.

1952 OLYMPICS

His wife, Dana, won gold in the javelin at the Helsinki Games.

To those who thought his running style looked clumsy, he said, "It's not gymnastics or figure skating, you know."

STRUGGLES

After his success, Emil Zátopek was made a colonel in the Czechoslovakian army, but was demoted in 1968 for criticizing the Soviet government. He struggled to find work and took a dangerous job in a uranium mine. He remained very popular and was officially given back his former status in 1990.

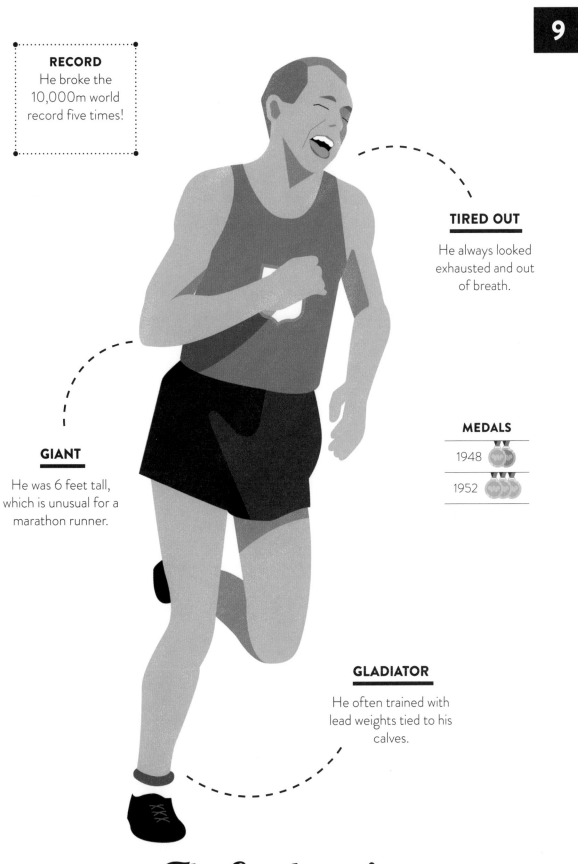

RECORD
He broke the 10,000m world record five times!

TIRED OUT
He always looked exhausted and out of breath.

GIANT
He was 6 feet tall, which is unusual for a marathon runner.

MEDALS

1948	
1952	

GLADIATOR
He often trained with lead weights tied to his calves.

The Czech engine

Marjorie Gestring

BIOGRAPHY

Nov 1922–
Apr 1992

American

Diving

3m springboard

Main rival:
Georgia Coleman
(American)

The queen of the diving board, Marjorie Gestring won gold in the 3m springboard in front of 15,000 spectators at the Berlin Olympics. At only 13, she is still the youngest ever Olympic champion. Although she won many other championships, she was never able to defend her Olympic title, as the 1940 and 1944 Games were canceled because of World War II.

UNBEATABLE

Her record will probably remain unbroken, as competitors now have to be at least 14.

AFTERWARDS

Marjorie Gestring tried to qualify for the London Olympics in 1948 but was unsuccessful. She was only 26!

1936 OLYMPICS

Three new sports were introduced: basketball, canoeing, and handball. This was the last time the Olympics staged a motor racing competition.

CHAMPION

Although she only competed in one Olympics due to world wars, she was US National Women's High Diving Champion in 1939, and retained the title in 1940.

RECORD
The youngest Olympic gold medal winner of all time.

MEDALS
1936

SUPERSTITIOUS
She always carried her teddy bear as a good luck charm.

EFFICIENT
Her dives were simple but perfectly executed.

WAR-TORN DREAMS
Many think she would have won more medals if the 1940 and 1944 Games had been held.

The youngest champion

Micheline Ostermeyer

BIOGRAPHY

Dec 1922–
Oct 2001

French

Athletics

Shot put, discus
throw, high jump

Main rival: Amelia
Piccinini (Italian)

In the build-up to the London Olympics in 1948, athlete and pianist Micheline Ostermeyer practiced much more on the piano than on the track, playing for five hours every day. But she still managed to win the discus by more than 75cm, and then, four days later, she won a second gold medal in the shot put. Finally, she finished third in the high jump, behind event specialists Alice Coachman from the US and Dorothy Tyler from Great Britain. A note-perfect performance all around.

PRIORITIES

She won the top piano prize at the National Conservatoire in Paris and dedicated herself to a career as a concert pianist. "I only did sport for fun," she said. "The piano was always my passion."

12

She won 12 French national titles in six different events: discus, shot put, high jump, 60m, 80m hurdles, and pentathlon.

PUTTING ON A SHOW

Micheline Ostermeyer was so happy about winning her first gold medal that she celebrated her victory by giving a Beethoven recital for the French team.

"The piano gives meaning and rhythm to my movement."

MEDALS

1948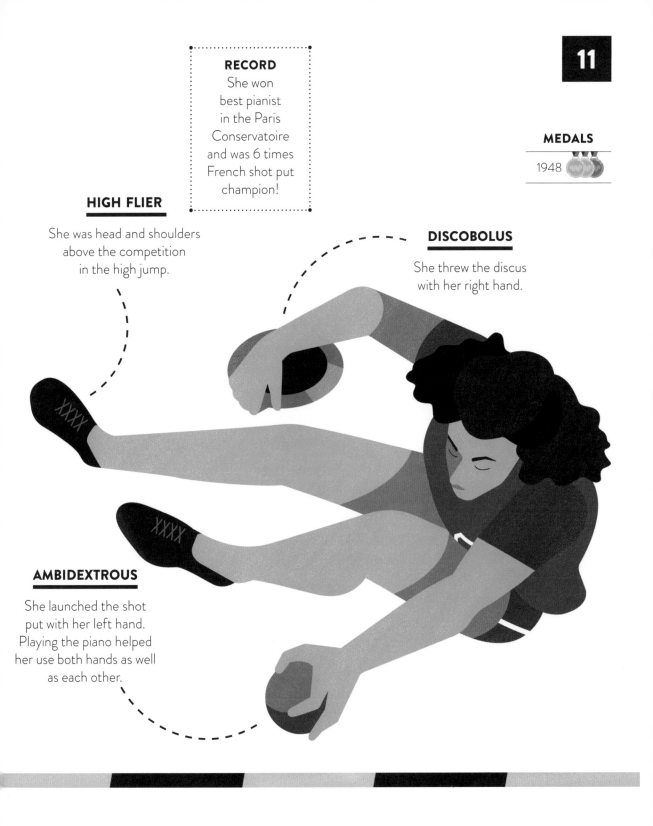

RECORD
She won best pianist in the Paris Conservatoire and was 6 times French shot put champion!

HIGH FLIER

She was head and shoulders above the competition in the high jump.

DISCOBOLUS

She threw the discus with her right hand.

AMBIDEXTROUS

She launched the shot put with her left hand. Playing the piano helped her use both hands as well as each other.

The virtuoso

Abebe Bikila

BIOGRAPHY

Aug 1932–
Oct 1973

Ethiopian

Athletics

Marathon

Main rival: Radhi
Ben Abdesselam
(Moroccan)

Abebe Bikila was an unknown athlete when he won the Rome marathon in 2 hours 15 minutes 16 seconds, beating the Olympic record. The Ethiopian athlete crossed the finish line beneath the Arch of Constantine, the exact spot from which Mussolini had sent out troops to invade his country 25 years earlier. Bikila was the first sub-Saharan African athlete to win a gold medal, and he opened the door for other African athletes who would come to dominate the sport. Four years later, in Tokyo, he became the first athlete to win the Olympic marathon for a second time.

HUMBLE BEGINNINGS

The son of a shepherd, as a child Abebe Bikila had to search the rolling hills around his village of Jato to find the best place for his family's flock of sheep to graze.

AFTERWARDS

In 1969, he was paralyzed in a serious accident, in a car that had been given to him by Ethiopian Emperor Haile Selassie.

1960 OLYMPICS

5,000 athletes from 83 countries took part: a new record because many former colonies had gained independence.

STROKE OF LUCK

Abebe Bikila wasn't originally selected for the Ethiopian team that went to the Rome Olympics, but he was called in to replace another athlete, Wami Biratu, who had been injured playing soccer.

RECORD
Only person to win Olympic gold in the marathon twice.

MEDALS
1960
1964

INDESTRUCTIBLE
He had his appendix taken out six weeks before his victory in Tokyo.

DISCIPLINED
He was a soldier in the Imperial Guard of Ethiopian Emperor Haile Selassie.

WITH OR WITHOUT SHOES
In Rome, he ran the marathon without shoes, but in Tokyo, he ran wearing sneakers.

The barefoot king

Betty Cuthbert

BIOGRAPHY

Apr 1938–
Aug 2017

Australian

Athletics

100m, 200m,
400m, 4x100m

Main rival:
Marlene Matthews
(Australian)

This Australian sprint specialist was the star of the Melbourne Olympics in 1956, at the age of just 18. She won gold in the 100m, 200m, and 4x100m relay, even setting a new world record. At the Tokyo Games in 1964, she won a fourth gold medal in the 400m, the first time female athletes competed in this event at the Olympics. But that wasn't all. She set 12 world records between 1956 and 1963, in distances ranging from 60m to 400m.

LACKING CONFIDENCE

Before the 1956 Games, Betty Cuthbert was convinced she wouldn't be selected for the Australian team. She even bought tickets to go to the athletics as a spectator!

1956 OLYMPICS

The International Olympic Committee forced East and West Germany to enter a united German team.

AFTERWARDS

Using a wheelchair due to a serious illness, Betty Cuthbert carried the Olympic torch at the opening ceremony of the Sydney Games in 2000.

PIONEER

This worldwide sporting legend was the first female athlete in history to win gold in all three sprint events: 100m, 200m, and 400m.

JAW-DROPPING
She often ran with her mouth open.

RECORD
The first sprinter to excel in all distances between 100 and 400m.

TEAM PLAYER
She ran in the sprint relay.

INJURED
She retired after the Rome Olympics in 1960 due to a hamstring injury.

MEDALS
1956
1964

Golden girl

Wilma Rudolph

BIOGRAPHY

Jun 1940–
Nov 1994

American

Athletics

100m, 200m,
4x100m

Main rival:
Marlene Matthews
(Australian)

Selected for the US Olympic team at just 16, Wilma Rudolph won a bronze medal at the Melbourne Games in 1956. But it was in Rome in 1960 that she earned her place as one of the true legends of the sport, becoming the first American woman to win three golds at a single Olympics. After her phenomenal success on the track, Wilma Rudolph retired and embarked on a career as a teacher and commentator.

OVERCOMING STRUGGLES

The seventeenth child of eighteen, Wilma Rudolph was born prematurely and was often ill as a child, but that only strengthened her champion's mentality!

1960 OLYMPICS

This was the first Olympics to be broadcast globally on TV.

AFTERWARDS

Rudolph and her mother were invited to the White House to meet newly elected president John F. Kennedy.

FIGHTING FOR RIGHTS

To celebrate her three Olympic titles, she made the governor of Tennessee organize a party that was open to everyone, no matter their origin or race.

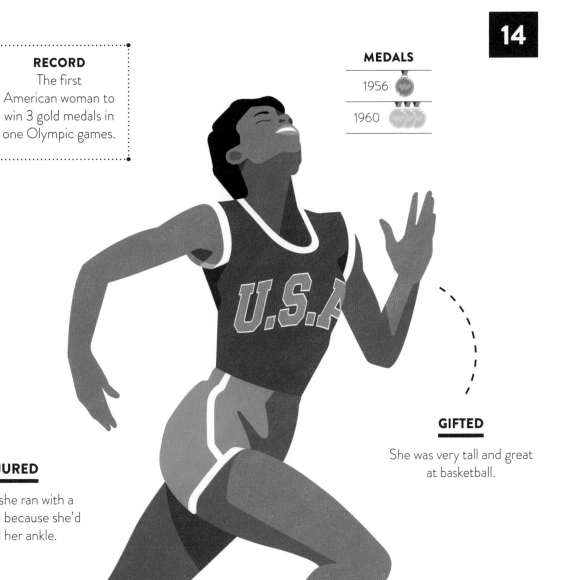

RECORD
The first American woman to win 3 gold medals in one Olympic games.

GIFTED

She was very tall and great at basketball.

INJURED

In Rome, she ran with a bandage on because she'd twisted her ankle.

CHILDHOOD ILLNESS

As a child she had polio, which weakened her leg and meant she wore a brace on it for five years.

The tornado

Tommie Smith

BIOGRAPHY

Jun 1944

American

Athletics

200m

Main rival: John Carlos (American)

A sociology student at San José University, Tommie Smith won a legendary 200m gold at the Mexico City Games, setting a world record of 19.83 seconds. But it was his medal ceremony that made history. With his compatriot John Carlos, he stood on the podium with his fist raised, wearing a black glove to protest against segregation in the US and show his support for the Black Power movement. Their protest was like a thunderbolt, coming six months after the assassination of Martin Luther King.

CHASED OUT

Tommie Smith and John Carlos were sent home by the president of the International Olympic Committee, who said their political gesture had no place at the Olympic Games. They were banned from competing by their federation.

9

The number of individual and team world records that Tommie Smith set between 1965 and 1968.

1968 OLYMPICS

"It only took a few seconds for America to make me an outcast, but they needed 35 years to transform me into a hero."

BELATED RECOGNITION

It wasn't until 2016 that Tommie Smith and John Carlos were honored for their activism, when Barack Obama invited them to a ceremony at the White House.

SOLEMN

He wore a serious expression and downcast eyes during his brave and dangerous political statement .

GLOVE

Symbol of black power

MEDALS

1968

BADGE

He wore the same one as the two other athletes on the podium. It said: "Olympic Project for Human Rights."

RECORD
This incredible athlete continues to campaign for human rights to this day.

Black panther

Mark Spitz

BIOGRAPHY

Feb 1950

American

Swimming

100m and 200m freestyle and butterfly

Main rival: Jerry Heidenreich (American)

Mark Spitz was very disappointed by his performance at the 1968 Games in Mexico, where he won two gold medals in the relays but none in the individual races. So he decided he was going to be the star of the pool in the Munich Olympics. And he kept his word, dominating the seven events he entered and breaking the world record in every single one! In his short career, the American swimmer set a total of 26 individual world records!

BIG TALKER

Before the Mexico City Olympics, at only 18, he announced that he was going to win six gold medals. He had to wait another four years, but he did even better than that!

1972 OLYMPICS

A terrorist group took athletes hostage in the Olympic village. Eleven athletes lost their lives.

AFTERWARDS

Feeling he would never top his 1968 performance, Mark Spitz retired from competition at only 22.

NUMBER TWO

For 36 years, Mark Spitz held the record for the most gold medals won at a single Games, but he was overtaken at the Beijing Olympics by his compatriot Michael Phelps.

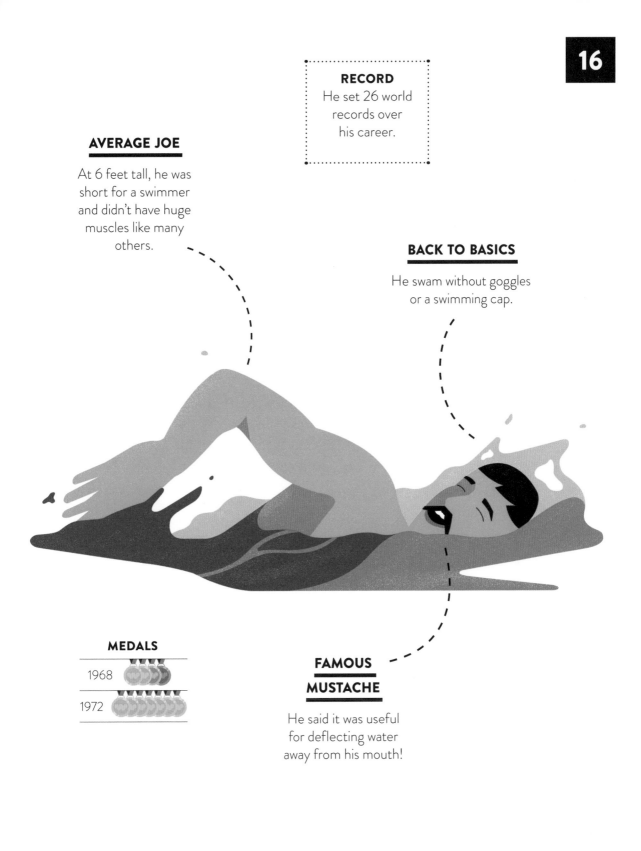

RECORD
He set 26 world records over his career.

AVERAGE JOE
At 6 feet tall, he was short for a swimmer and didn't have huge muscles like many others.

BACK TO BASICS
He swam without goggles or a swimming cap.

MEDALS
1968
1972

FAMOUS MUSTACHE
He said it was useful for deflecting water away from his mouth!

The torpedo

Daley Thompson

BIOGRAPHY

Jul 1958

British

Decathlon

Main rival: Jürgen Hingsen (West German)

Born in London to a Nigerian father and a Scottish mother, this decathlon specialist competed at his first Olympics in 1976, when he was just 18. Four years later, he won gold in Moscow, then successfully defended his title in Los Angeles, becoming the first athlete to retain his decathlon title since the American Bob Mathias at the 1952 Games in Helsinki. An all-arounder, especially gifted at the running and jumping events, he is known for his competitive spirit and strong character.

SUPERSTAR

In 1984, he became the first athlete to have his own video game. Players compete in the ten decathlon disciplines and are eliminated if they don't perform well enough.

8,847

That's how many points he scored when he set his world record in 1984, a performance that remained unbeaten for 8 years.

THE EVENT

The decathlon has 10 events: 4 running races (100m, 400m, 110m hurdles, 1500m), 3 jumps (long jump, high jump, pole vault), and 3 throws (shot put, discus javelin).

UNBEATABLE

Between 1979 and 1987, he won the decathlon at every official competition. He won the world championships in Helsinki in 1983 and the European title in 1982 and 1986.

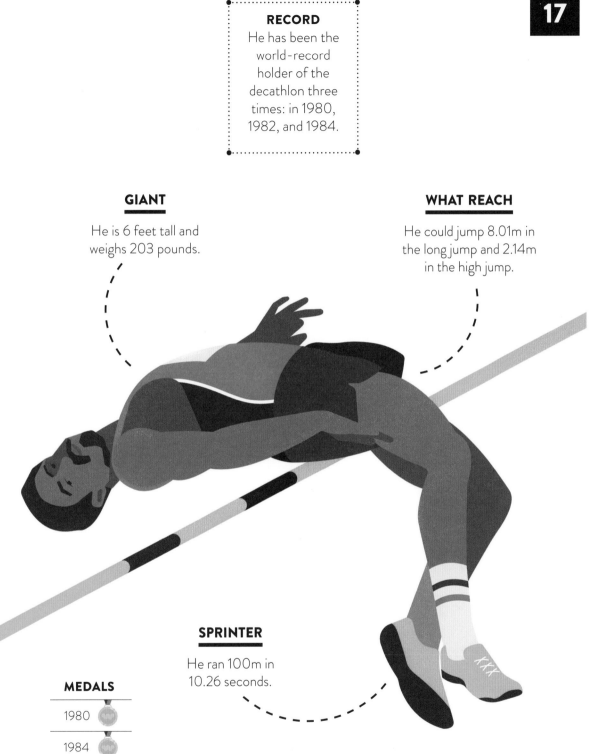

GIANT

He is 6 feet tall and weighs 203 pounds.

WHAT REACH

He could jump 8.01m in the long jump and 2.14m in the high jump.

SPRINTER

He ran 100m in 10.26 seconds.

MEDALS

1980	
1984	

The gladiator

Carl Lewis

BIOGRAPHY

Jul 1961

American

Athletics

100m, 200m, long jump, 4x100m

Main rivals: Linford Christie (British) and Mike Powell (American)

This Olympic hero was an extraordinary athlete with a powerful, elegant running style. At the Los Angeles Games in 1984, the American won the 100m, long jump, and 200m, then topped it all off with a gold medal in the 4x100m relay. His feat equaled the achievements of Jesse Owens, who had been his childhood hero and victor at the 1936 Berlin Games. Carl Lewis competed at three more Olympics, winning five more golds and a silver.

UNIQUE

With four consecutive Olympic long jump golds, Carl Lewis is the only athlete who has won this event at more than one Olympics. He has nine Olympic golds, eight world titles, and 11 world records.

FIGHTING SPIRIT

By 1994, Lewis had lost some of his speed, and he only qualified for the long jump at the Atlanta Olympics. He scraped into the final on his third attempt, but then won gold!

"If you don't have confidence, you'll always find a way not to win."

65

Between 1981 and 1991, he won the long jump in 65 consecutive meets.

RECORD
The world record breaker in the 100m in 1991, 4x100m in 1992, 200m in 1983, and the long jump in 1991.

STYLISH
He had pride his appearance and had a fresh buzz cut for the 1984 Games.

MEDALS
1984	
1988	
1992	
1996	

SLENDER
This elegant sprinter is 6'2" tall.

STAR POWER
He had his name stitched onto his socks in gold thread.

King Carl

Nadia Comăneci

BIOGRAPHY

Nov 1961

Romanian,
then American

Gymnastics

Floor exercise,
vault,
uneven bars,
beam

Main rival:
Nellie Kim
(Soviet)

Child prodigy Nadia Comăneci burst onto the scene at the Montreal Games in 1976. At just 14, she was the first gymnast in Olympic history to be awarded a perfect score of 10. She won three gold medals (in the uneven bars, the all-around competition, and the beam), one silver (in the team competition), and a bronze (on the floor). Four years later, she won two more golds in Moscow, but finished second in the all-around competition behind Soviet gymnast Yelena Davydova.

> "You don't compete for a score. You are in competition with yourself to do your best."

1976 OLYMPICS

Canada didn't win a single gold medal! It was the first time in Olympic history that a host nation failed to win gold.

COMMUNIST ICON

In Romania, Nadia Comăneci was a symbol of the triumph of communism over capitalism. Nicolae Ceaușescu, who ruled the country with an iron fist, awarded her the prestigious title of Hero of Socialist Labour.

GOLDEN COUPLE

After retiring, Comăneci fled to the United States in 1989. She married Bart Conner, an American gymnast and double gold medallist at the Los Angeles Olympics (1984).

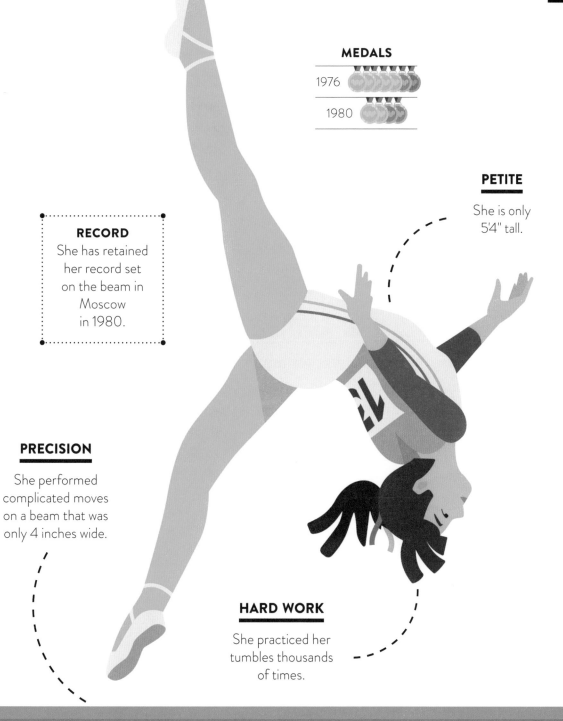

MEDALS

1976

1980

PETITE

She is only
5'4" tall.

RECORD

She has retained
her record set
on the beam in
Moscow
in 1980.

PRECISION

She performed
complicated moves
on a beam that was
only 4 inches wide.

HARD WORK

She practiced her
tumbles thousands
of times.

The perfectionist

Birgit Fischer

BIOGRAPHY

Feb 1962

German

Kayaking

Main rival:
Vanja Gesheva
(Bulgarian)

The only woman to have won a gold medal at six different Olympic Games, this kayaker set her incredible record when representing first East Germany, then the united Germany. She is also the only woman to have won Olympic medals 20 years apart. Her collection could have been even more impressive but she couldn't compete at the Los Angeles Olympics in 1984 because most of the Eastern Bloc countries boycotted the Games.

INEXHAUSTIBLE

Her father, a keen kayaker, taught her and her two brothers on the River Havel. At six years old, she already showed incredible talent. At 18, she was the youngest ever Olympic kayak champion, and at 42, she was the oldest!

35

She won 35 medals at the world championships between 1979 and 1988. Twenty-seven of them were gold!

AFTERWARDS

Birgit Fischer wanted to compete at the London Olympics in 2012, but her cardiologists advised her against it, as it would put too much strain on her body.

WHAT A FAMILY

Her brother Frank was a multiple world kayak champion and her niece Fanny won gold at the Beijing Olympics in 2008. Her sister-in-law, swimmer Sarina Hülsenbeck, won a gold medal at the Moscow Olympics in 1980.

RECORD

She is the second most decorated medalist in the Games after Russian gymnast Larisa Latynina.

MEDALS

1980	
1988	
1992	
1996	
1996	
2000	
2004	

EXPERT

She handles her double-bladed paddle with a lot of skill.

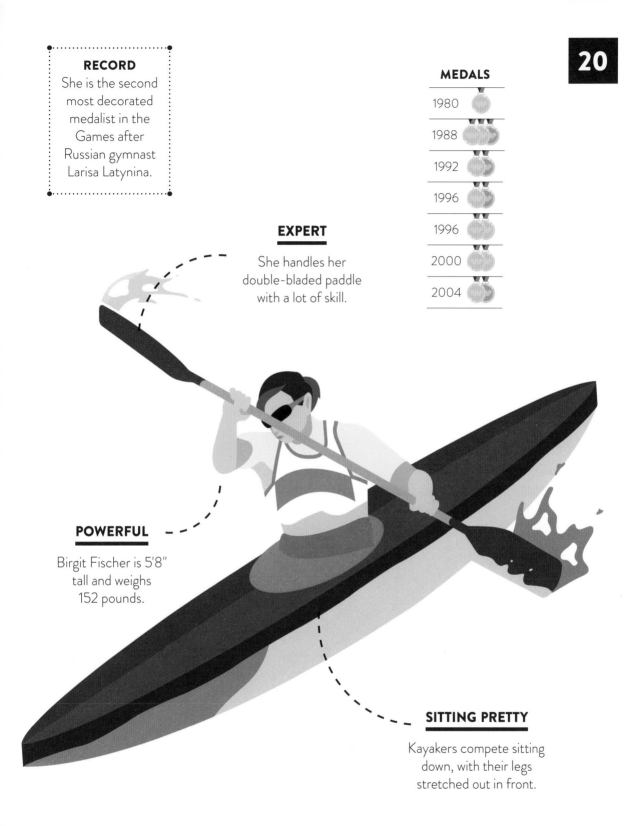

POWERFUL

Birgit Fischer is 5'8" tall and weighs 152 pounds.

SITTING PRETTY

Kayakers compete sitting down, with their legs stretched out in front.

Superwoman

Steve Redgrave

BIOGRAPHY

Mar 1962

British

Rowing

Coxed four, coxless four, and coxless pairs

Main rivals: Carmine and Giuseppe Abbagnale (Italian)

The greatest rower of all time, this British athlete won gold at five consecutive Olympics, from Los Angeles in 1984 to Sydney in 2000. Five Olympics, five gold medals! Driven by an incredible competitive spirit and will to win, Steve Redgrave dominated international competitions for years. As well as his Olympic titles, he won nine world championships.

WATCH WHAT YOU SAY

After winning his fourth gold medal in 1996, Steve Redgrave announced his retirement, saying, "Anybody who sees me in a boat has my permission to shoot me." Dangerous words, as he later returned to competitive rowing!

2000 OLYMPICS

He won gold in his final Olympic appearance in 2000 in Sydney at the Games of the new Millennium.

AFTERWARDS

In 2001, he was knighted by Queen Elizabeth II at Buckingham Palace. He is now Sir Steve Redgrave.

BRITISH HERO

He was the final torchbearer at the opening ceremony of the London Games in 2012 and handed the torch over to future stars of British sports for them to light the Olympic cauldron.

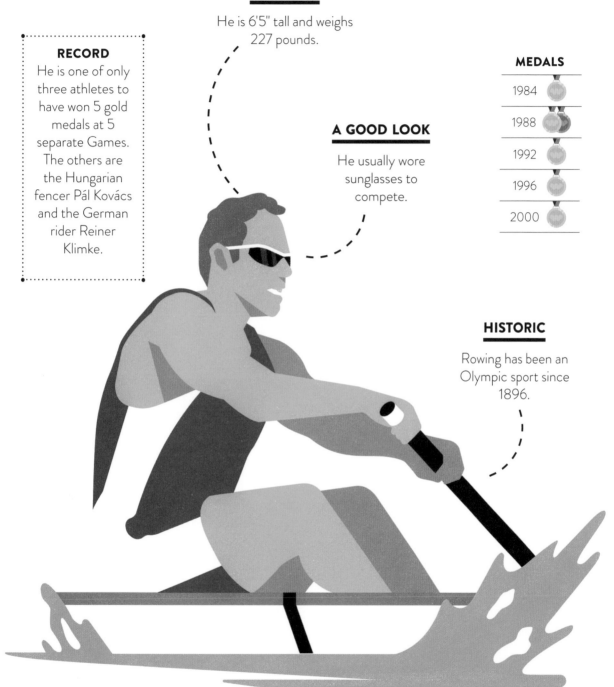

HERCULES
He is 6'5" tall and weighs 227 pounds.

RECORD
He is one of only three athletes to have won 5 gold medals at 5 separate Games. The others are the Hungarian fencer Pál Kovács and the German rider Reiner Klimke.

A GOOD LOOK
He usually wore sunglasses to compete.

MEDALS
1984
1988
1992
1996
2000

HISTORIC
Rowing has been an Olympic sport since 1896.

King of the water

Nawal El Moutawakel

BIOGRAPHY

Apr 1962

Moroccan

Athletics

400m hurdles

Main rival: Judi Brown (American)

At the Los Angeles Games in 1984, this 22-year-old Moroccan surprised the crowds by winning the 400m hurdles by a comfortable distance. She earned her place in the history books as the first African, Arab, and Muslim woman to win a gold medal at the Olympics. A superstar in her country, Nawal El Moutawakel won many African titles before she left her shorts and running shoes in the locker room and embarked on a completely new career as a coach and politician.

ROLE MODEL

Nawal El Moutawakel was an inspirational icon for millions of young Muslim women.

NATIONAL CELEBRATIONS

The 400m hurdles final was shown live at 2 o'clock in the morning. After her victory, crowds took to the streets of Casablanca, her home town, to celebrate their heroine.

AFTERWARDS

A committed feminist, Nawal El Moutawakel became vice president of the International Olympic Committee, as well as Minister of Sports in Morocco!

"I started hurdles at 15, in 1977, and very quickly I beat all the Moroccan records in my category. I ran barefoot and beat all the boys."

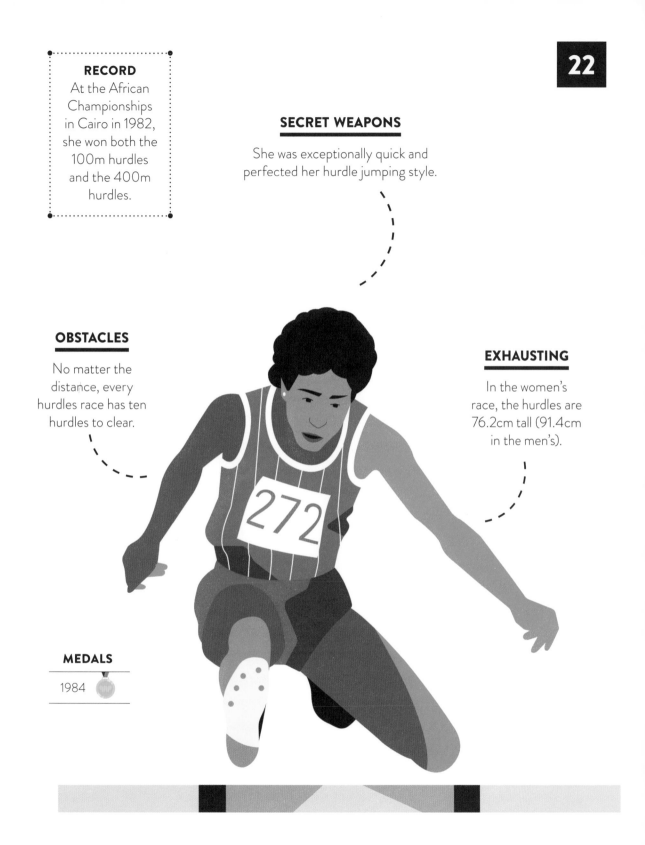

22

RECORD

At the African Championships in Cairo in 1982, she won both the 100m hurdles and the 400m hurdles.

SECRET WEAPONS

She was exceptionally quick and perfected her hurdle jumping style.

OBSTACLES

No matter the distance, every hurdles race has ten hurdles to clear.

EXHAUSTING

In the women's race, the hurdles are 76.2cm tall (91.4cm in the men's).

MEDALS

1984

National hero

Trischa Zorn

BIOGRAPHY

Jun 1964

American

Swimming

50m, 100m, and 200m backstroke; 200m and 400m medley; 200m breaststroke; 4x50m medley relay; 4x50m freestyle relay

This American swimmer was born blind, but that didn't stop her from competing at the Paralympics in 1980, 1984, 1988, 1992, 1996, 2000, and 2004—that's seven consecutive Games! At the Seoul and Barcelona Paralympics, she left the rest of the field in her wake, winning 24 medals, including 22 golds. A fierce competitor, Trischa Zorn finished her career as the most decorated summer Paralympian of all time, having won more than 50 medals in the pool.

HONORS

Trischa Zorn was selected to read the athletes' oath at the 1996 Paralympic Games. She was also chosen as her country's flagbearer at the closing ceremony of the Athens Games in 2004.

AFTERWARDS

USA Swimming's prize for disabled athletes, awarded each year, was named after her.

ROLE MODEL

Trischa Zorn studied education and law at the University of Nebraska. In 2001, she also began teaching children with special needs alongside her coaching activities.

> "My motivation lies in the fact that I truly love what I'm doing."

23

GOLDEN GIRL

At three Paralympic Games, she won only golds in individual events.

RECORD

During her career, she broke the world record in nearly all swimming events she took part in.

STAYING POWER

She competed at her first Games at the age of 16, and her last at the age of 40.

PAYING HOMAGE

She dedicated her last medal, a bronze, to her mother, who had died shortly before the Games.

MEDALS

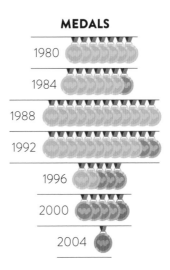

1980
1984
1988
1992
1996
2000
2004

Queen of the pool

Jonas Jacobsson

BIOGRAPHY

Jun 1965

Swedish

Shooting

Main rival: Doron Shaziri (Israeli)

This Swedish athlete was born paralyzed from the waist down and uses a wheelchair. He took up shooting at the age of seven and has competed at nine consecutive summer Paralympics, from 1980 to 2012, winning a medal at every Games. With 30 medals to his name, including 17 golds, Jonas Jacobsson is the most decorated male athlete in the history of the Paralympics.

PRECOCIOUS

Most athletes who compete in this sport are older, but Jacobsson competed at his first Paralympics, in Arnhem in 1980, at just 15 years old! He wasn't intimidated by the competition, and won a silver and bronze medal!

THE EVENT

Depending on their disability, shooters have a choice of lying down, sitting, or standing while they aim at the target.

"To be good at something strengthens self-confidence, but it is important to have a humble attitude at the same time."

ANOTHER SHOOTING LEGEND

British athlete Isabel Newstead also earned her place in Paralympic history by winning 18 medals in three completely different events (four in shooting, nine in swimming, and five in track and field).

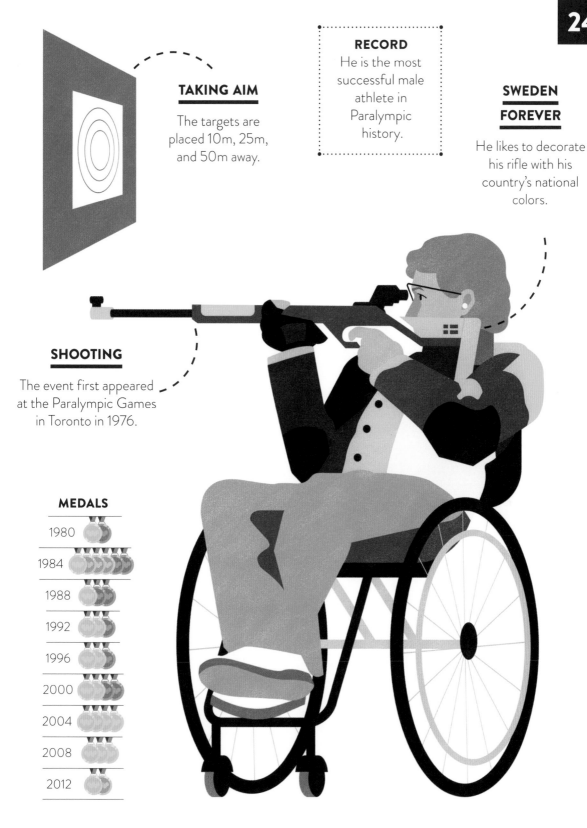

24

TAKING AIM

The targets are placed 10m, 25m, and 50m away.

RECORD

He is the most successful male athlete in Paralympic history.

SWEDEN FOREVER

He likes to decorate his rifle with his country's national colors.

SHOOTING

The event first appeared at the Paralympic Games in Toronto in 1976.

MEDALS

1980

1984

1988

1992

1996

2000

2004

2008

2012

Sharp shooter

Sebastian Coe

BIOGRAPHY

Sep 1965

British

Athletics

800m, 1500m

Main rival: Steve Ovett (British)

As **world record holder**, British runner Sebastian Coe was the clear favorite for the 800m gold at the 1980 Olympics in Moscow. But he ran what he called "the worst race of my life" and finished second behind his rival Steve Ovett. Six days later, he got his revenge, winning the 1500m. Four years later, history repeated itself. Sebastian Coe finished second in the 800m and won the 1500m with a lead of 6 meters. He is the only athlete to have twice won gold at this distance.

KEEPING IT IN THE FAMILY

From a young age, Sebastian Coe was coached by his own father, who had very high expectations and took training, and winning, very seriously indeed.

1980 OLYMPICS

The United States and around 50 other nations boycotted the Games following the USSR's invasion of Afghanistan in 1979.

9

The number of world records beaten by Sebastian Coe: 800m, 1000m, 1500m, mile, and 4x800m.

BORN LEADER

The king of middle-distance running has also excelled off the track: he was an MP in the House of Commons, chairman of the London Olympics in 2012, knighted by the queen, and has been president of the International Association of Athletics Federations since 2015.

25

RECORD
Since 2015 he has chaired the International Association of Athletics Federations (called 'World Athletics' since 2019).

GOOD COACH
His father helped improve his running technique.

PERFECT PHYSIQUE
Sebastian Coe has a slim build but very muscular legs.

CLASS ACT
His running style looked graceful and effortless.

254

MEDALS
1980
1984

Lord of the rings

Michael Johnson

BIOGRAPHY

Sep 1967

American

Athletics

200m, 400m, 4x400m

Main rival: Frankie Fredericks (Namibian)

Michael Johnson won his first Olympic gold in the 4x400m relay at the Barcelona Games in 1992, but he reached new heights at the next Olympics in Atlanta in 1996, becoming the first male athlete to win the double in the 200m and 400m. He successfully defended his 400m title four years later in Sydney, and became known for his incredible speed, distinctive running style, and long career.

SERIOUS

As a young man, Michael Johnson focused on his studies at Baylor University in Waco, Texas, and sports were just for fun. Once he'd finished his accounting degree, he became a full-time athlete in 1990.

58

Between 1990 and 1997, Michael Johnson was unbeaten in the 400m, winning 58 consecutive races.

AFTERWARDS

He became a sports commentator and manager for athlete Jeremy Wariner, who won 400m gold in Athens in 2004.

RECORD BREAKER

At the world championships in 1993, he set a new world record, running the 400m in 43.18 seconds. The record stood for 17 years. In the 200m final at the Atlanta Games, he finished in 19.32 seconds, setting a world record that was only broken 12 years later by Usain Bolt.

26

STATUESQUE

He stood very straight when running, even leaning back a little.

RECORD

He broke world records in the 200m and 4x400m relay in 1993 and the 400m in 1996.

MEDALS

1992	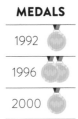
1996	
2000	

SHORT STRIDES

His feet hardly seemed to leave the track.

GOLDEN BOY

He wore gold sneakers when he won his incredible double.

Superman

Marie-José Pérec

BIOGRAPHY

May 1968

French

Athletics

200m, 400m, 4x400m, 400m hurdles

Main rival: Merlene Ottey (Jamaican)

With her victory in Barcelona, this sprinting queen became only the second female French athlete to win an Olympic gold in the 400m, after Colette Besson. And that was just for starters. At the Atlanta Games in 1996, she successfully defended her Olympic 400m title, the first time this had been done by any athlete, male or female. Three days later, the Guadeloupean won gold in the 200m, ahead of Jamaican Merlene Ottey. She is the only female French triple Olympic champion, a true legend of the Games.

1992 OLYMPICS

For the first time, NBA players were allowed to compete in basketball. Michael Jordan and Charles Barkley helped bring home gold for the US dream team.

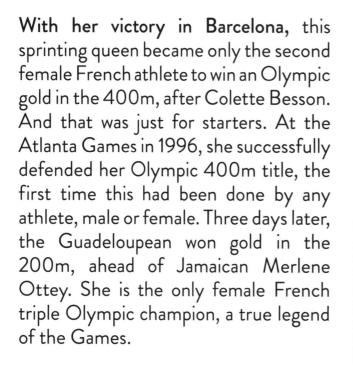

RECORD HOLDER

More than 20 years after she set them, Marie-José Pérec's French national records in the 200m (21.99s, 1996), 400m (48.25s, 1996), 400m hurdles (53.21s, 1995), and 4x400m (3 min 22.34s, 1994) remain unbeaten.

A RUNNING GREAT

She is only the second female runner in history to have won the 400m and 200m at the same Olympics. American athlete Valerie Brisco-Hooks achieved this at the Los Angeles Games in 1984, but athletes from the Eastern Bloc didn't compete that year because of the boycott.

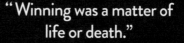

"Winning was a matter of life or death."

27

BREATHLESS

In the 1992 final, she stopped breathing for nine strides to try and make herself go faster.

RECORD
Marie-José Pérec is the only French athlete to have won three gold medals at the Olympic Games.

SLENDER

She is slim but incredibly powerful.

MEDALS

1992

1996

LONG LEGS

She could cover 2.2m (more than 7 feet) in one stride.

The gazelle

Michael Edgson

BIOGRAPHY

May 1969

Canadian

Swimming

Butterfly, freestyle, backstroke, medley

As a young athlete, Michael Edgson loved hockey, soccer, and gymnastics, but he decided to concentrate on swimming. It turned out to be a good choice. At just 15 years old, the visually impaired athlete represented Canada at the Paralympics in 1984. At the Seoul Games in 1988, he reached the pinnacle of his career, winning nine golds and setting four world records. When he retired from competition, he'd won 21 medals, 18 of which were gold.

EARLY RETIREMENT

Although he could have won more medals, Michael Edgson decided to retire from competitive swimming after the 1992 Paralympics in Barcelona. He was only 23 years old!

AFTERWARDS

A brilliant student from the University of Victoria, Michael Edgson became CFO of the Canadian Paralympic Committee after his athletic career.

FINALLY!

In 1988, Seoul played host first to the 8,391 Olympic athletes, then to the 3,053 Paralympic athletes two weeks later. It was the first time since 1964 that both competitions were held in the same city.

9

He set nine world records at three different Paralympic Games.

28

RECORD
He broke 20 world records in disabled sports during his career.

MEDALS

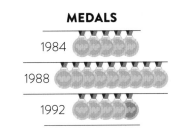

1984

1988

1992

SUPER FAST
He was particularly good at the 200m butterfly.

PIONEERING
PARALYMPIC SPORT
Swimming has been a Paralympic sport since the first Games in 1960.

PATRIOTIC
He has a maple leaf— the symbol of Canada— tattooed on his chest.

The dolphin

Isabell Werth

BIOGRAPHY

Jul 1969

German

Horse riding

Dressage

Main rival:
Charlotte Dujardin
(British)

This German dressage star competed at the Barcelona Games in 1992, the Atlanta Games in 1996, the Sydney Games in 2000, the Athens Games in 2004, the Beijing Games in 2008, and the Rio Games in 2016. She didn't compete at the London Olympics in 2012 because her top-ranked horse, Don Johnson, was injured in the qualifiers. Over 24 years, Isabell Werth won ten Olympic medals, both with the German team and in individual events. She also won the world championships seven times and the European championships nine times.

LOYAL PARTNER

For many years, Isabell Werth rode a liver chestnut gelding named Gigolo. They won four gold medals and two silvers together at the Olympic Games, as well as four world titles.

THE EVENT

Equestrian events are the only Olympic sport where men and women compete against each other, at least until 2020.

AFTERWARDS

She has launched a brand of equestrian accessories (including riding clothes and saddles) but is still competing.

MULTI-TALENTED

The gifted rider combined competing with studying for a law degree. She worked for some time as a lawyer, then in marketing.

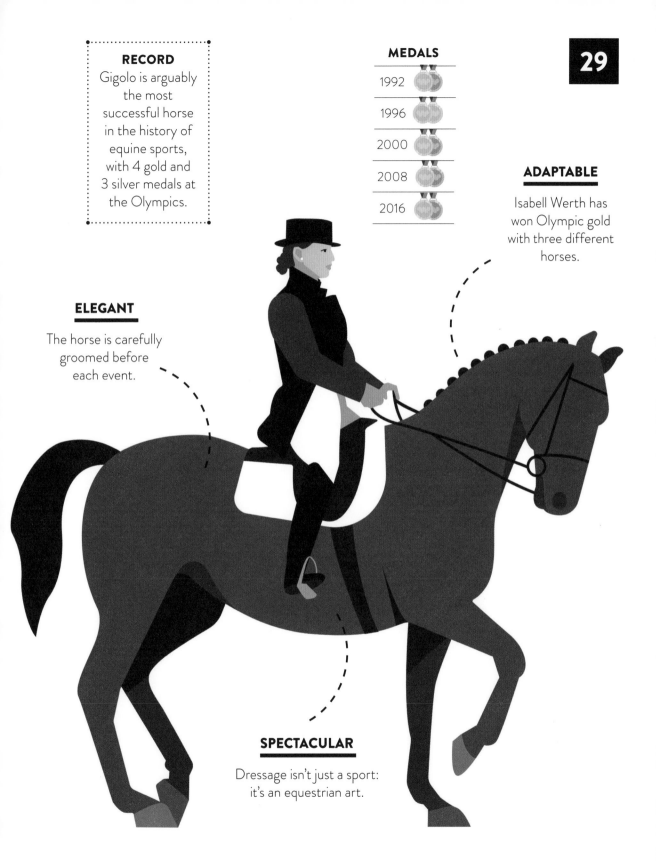

RECORD

Gigolo is arguably the most successful horse in the history of equine sports, with 4 gold and 3 silver medals at the Olympics.

MEDALS

1992	
1996	
2000	
2008	
2016	

29

ADAPTABLE

Isabell Werth has won Olympic gold with three different horses.

ELEGANT

The horse is carefully groomed before each event.

SPECTACULAR

Dressage isn't just a sport: it's an equestrian art.

The elegant rider

Maria Mutola

BIOGRAPHY

Oct 1972

Mozambican

Athletics

800m

Main rival: Ana Fidelia Quirot (Cuban) and Stephanie Graf (Austrian)

As a child this young Mozambican first played soccer, then switched to 800m running. This talented young athlete went to her first Olympics in Seoul at the age of just 16. Eight years later, she won bronze in Atlanta, then won Mozambique's first ever gold medal in Sydney in 2000. But she didn't stop there, placing fourth at the Athens Olympics in 2004 and fifth in Beijing in 2008.

GENEROUS

In 2003, she earned a million dollars when she was unbeaten in the six most important meets of the year. She used some of this money to set up sports projects for underprivileged children in her home country.

10

Maria Mutola won three world outdoor titles (1993, 2001, 2003) and seven indoor titles (1993, 1995, 1997, 2001, 2003, 2004, 2006).

AFTERWARDS

Maria Mutola played for the Mozambique soccer team at the All-Africa Games in 2011 and scored a goal against Algeria.

NATIONAL HERO

When she returned to Maputo after winning her Olympic title, Maria Mutola was greeted by cheering crowds. A street in the capital city was named after her.

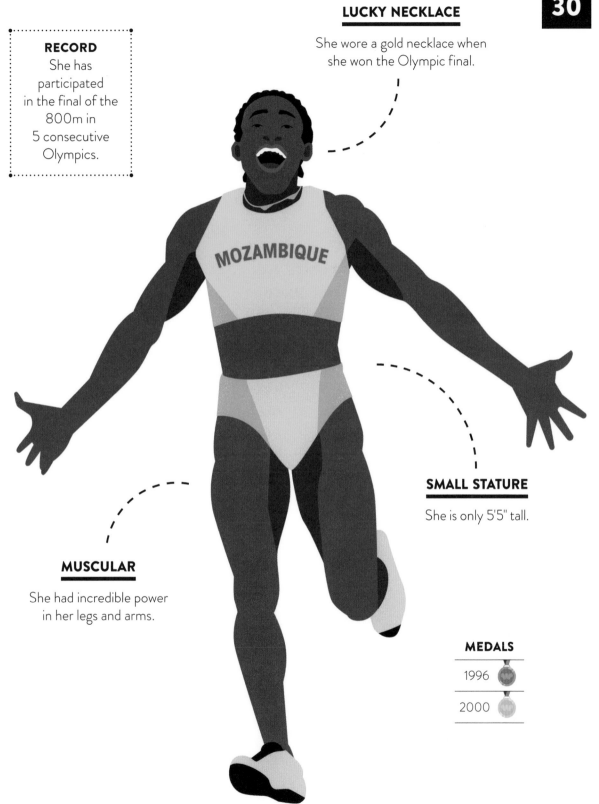

30

LUCKY NECKLACE

She wore a gold necklace when she won the Olympic final.

RECORD
She has participated in the final of the 800m in 5 consecutive Olympics.

MOZAMBIQUE

SMALL STATURE

She is only 5'5" tall.

MUSCULAR

She had incredible power in her legs and arms.

MEDALS

| 1996 | 🥈 |
| 2000 | 🥇 |

Maputo express

Cathy Freeman

BIOGRAPHY

Feb 1973

Australian

Athletics

400m

Main rival:
Marie-José Pérec
(French)

First Nations runner Cathy Freeman was a rising star of Australian athletics in the 1990s. She won silver in the 400m at the Atlanta Games in 1996, losing out to Marie-José Pérec, but took her revenge in spectacular style. She took home the world title in 1997 and 1998, and won Olympic gold in front of a cheering home crowd at the Sydney Games in 2000.

POLITICAL

Cathy Freeman called on the Australian government to issue an official apology for the policy of removing First Nations children from their families and placing them with white parents. Her own grandmother was part of this "stolen generation."

AFTERWARDS

In 2007, she set up a foundation to improve education for First Nations children.

"I felt the track beneath my feet and I'll never forget how it felt like I was being carried along, like a surfer riding a wave."

SYMBOLIC

At the Sydney Games, Cathy Freeman was chosen to light the Olympic flame, an unexpected honor, as it was usually sporting heroes from the past who lit the Olympic cauldron.

31

RECORD

The IOC allowed her to sport an unofficial flag after her victory in 2000, which is normally forbidden.

COVERED UP

Cathy wore a full tracksuit and hood when she won her Olympic title.

PROUD

She ran her victory lap holding an Australian flag and an Aboriginal flag.

EMOTIONAL

At the end of the race, she was almost in tears.

MEDALS

| 1996 |  |
| 2000 | |

Aboriginal hero

Valentina Vezzali

BIOGRAPHY

Feb 1974

Italian

Fencing

Fleuret

Main rival: Nam Hyun-Hee (South Korean)

This Italian fencing legend won her third gold medal at the Beijing Olympics in 2008, becoming the first fencer, male or female, to win three consecutive individual titles in any event (épée, foil, or saber). This incredibly gifted and determined athlete also won three Olympic golds in the team competition (1996, 2000, 2012).

FIGHTER

At the London Olympics in 2012, the Italian was trailing by four touches with only 13 seconds left in the bronze medal match. She fought back to win her final individual medal.

10

As well as her Olympic medals, she has won the Women's Foil World Cup a record 10 times between 1996 and 2008.

AFTERWARDS

Valentina Vezzali pursued a political career and was elected as an Italian MP in 2013.

AN OLYMPIC SPORT

Fencing has been an Olympic sport since the first modern Games in 1896, when men competed in the foil and saber. Women had to wait until 1924 to compete in the foil, 1996 for the épée, and 2004 for the saber.

32

RECORD
She is the most successful fencer in history.

IMPRESSIVE
She was nicknamed "the boa constrictor" by her competitors.

SKILLFUL
She used her right arm to fend off opponents.

TOUGH
She had to have surgery on her left knee halfway through her career.

MEDALS

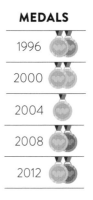

1996	
2000	
2004	
2008	
2012	

The signorina

Tony Estanguet

BIOGRAPHY

May 1978

French

Canoe

C1 slalom (individual in whitewater)

Main rival: Michal Martikán (Slovakian)

Tony Estanguet was a surprise champion in Sydney in 2000, but his victory was expected in Athens in 2004, when he became the first slalom canoeist to successfully defend his Olympic title. At the Beijing Olympics, he suffered a disappointing defeat, but that was not the end of Tony Estanguet. Four years later, he completed a penalty-free run in the canoe slalom at the London Olympics , securing his place in French sports history.

SIBLING RIVALRY

The French canoeist dedicated his first Olympic gold to his brother Patrice, who had won bronze in Atlanta. He had defeated him at the French trials.

> "I am very proud to have competed four times and to have been my country's flagbearer."

AFTERWARDS

Tony Estanguet is the president of the Organizing Committee for the Paris Olympics in 2024.

MAN ON A MISSION

When he retired from competition with three Olympic golds, three world titles and three European titles, Tony Estanguet was immediately elected to the International Olympic Committee.

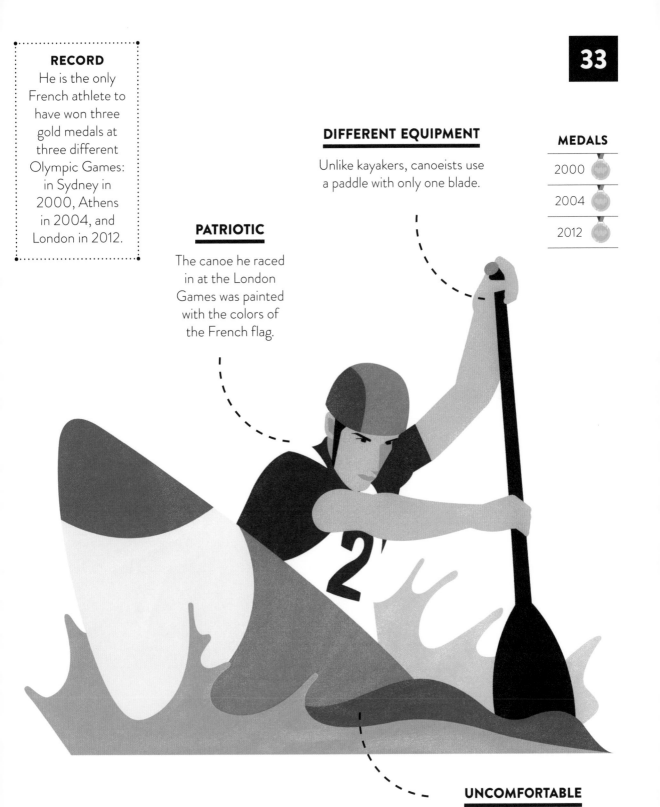

33

RECORD

He is the only French athlete to have won three gold medals at three different Olympic Games: in Sydney in 2000, Athens in 2004, and London in 2012.

DIFFERENT EQUIPMENT

Unlike kayakers, canoeists use a paddle with only one blade.

MEDALS

2000

2004

2012

PATRIOTIC

The canoe he raced in at the London Games was painted with the colors of the French flag.

UNCOMFORTABLE

In a canoe, competitors kneel instead of sit.

The boss

Yelena Isinbayeva

BIOGRAPHY

Jun 1982

Russian

Athletics

Pole vault

Main rival: Svetlana Feofanova (Russian)

The Russian took up pole vaulting in 1998 and won her first international title six months later at the World Youth Games. Five years later, she set her first world record, clearing 4.82m, and established herself as the greatest female pole vaulter of all time. Between 2004 and 2008, Yelena Isinbayeva won almost every competition she took part in and took home two gold medals at the Athens and Beijing Olympics.

TOO TALL

Yelena Isinbayeva wanted to be a gymnast, but she had to give up the sport because she was too tall. At the age of 15, she was more than 5'7' tall, so she changed sports and discovered her incredible talent for pole vaulting.

17

Between 2003 and 2009, Yelena Isinbayeva beat the world record 17 times, at heights ranging from 4.81m to 5.06m.

THE EVENT

Pole vault has been an Olympic event for men since 1896. Women first competed in it at the Sydney Games in 2000, where American Stacy Dragila took home gold.

THE NAME'S ISINBAYEVA, YELENA ISINBAYEVA

The athlete didn't want to rule out any possibilities for her retirement. After winning gold in Beijing, she said, "I'd like to go into cinema. My dream is to be in a James Bond film."

34

RECORD
Between 2003 and 2009, she broke the pole vault world record 17 times.

MEDALS

2004	🥇
2008	🥇
2012	🥉

LIGHT
She only weighs 143 pounds, so she could fly through the air.

CHATTY
Before each jump, she talked to her pole to help her concentrate.

STYLISH
She liked to have her nails painted for competitions.

The tsarina

Mo Farah

BIOGRAPHY

Mar 1983

British

Athletics

5000m, 10,000m

Main rival: Kenenisa Bekele (Ethiopian)

After moving to the UK from Somalia at the age of eight, as a teenager Mo Farah impressed on the athletics track, developing a talent for sprint finishes that is very rare in middle-distance runners. He became Olympic champion in the 10,000m and 5000m at the London Games in 2012, then repeated the feat four years later, winning gold again over the same distances in Rio in 2016. The only other Olympian to have achieved this double is the Finnish athlete Lasse Virén, who won his golds in 1972 and 1976.

ROYAL RECOGNITION

As the most decorated British track athlete of all time, Mohamed "Mo" Farah was knighted by Queen Elizabeth II in 2017. Also being honored at Buckingham Palace on that day was Scottish tennis player and two-time Wimbledon champion Andy Murray.

6

Mo Farah has won six world titles: three in the 5000m (2011, 2013, and 2015) and three in the 10,000m (2013, 2015, and 2017).

AFTERWARDS

Farah decided to compete in the marathon and won the event in Chicago in 2018, beating the European record with a time of 2 hrs 5 min 11 s.

CHILDHOOD AMBITIONS

Before his PE teacher recognized Farah's talent, Mo had two dreams: he wanted to be a car mechanic or to play on the right wing for Arsenal.

35

THE MOBOT

Farah celebrates his victories with his signature pose, forming the letter "M," the first letter of his name.

MEDALS

| 2012 | |
| 2016 | |

RECORD
He holds the world record for the indoor 2-mile race.

GREAT BRITAIN

ROCK STAR

He wore sunglasses when he won the 5000m at the London Olympics.

SLENDER FRAME

He has very slim legs and only weighs 130 pounds.

The king

Michael Phelps

BIOGRAPHY

Jun 1985

American

Swimming

Freestyle, butterfly, and medley

Main rival: Milorad Čavić (Serbian)

A specialist in butterfly, freestyle, and individual medley, Michael Phelps is the most decorated Olympian in history, with 28 medals, including 23 golds. At the Athens and Rio Games in 2004 and 2008, the American outclassed the rest of the field, winning medals and setting incredible times. In 2008, the Baltimore native entered eight events at the Beijing Olympics. He won every single one and set seven new world records!

ENERGY

Diagnosed with ADHD as a child, Michael Phelps took up swimming at the age of seven to burn off some of his extra energy. He was clearly talented, winning all the youth categories in his events.

"You can't put a limit to anything. The more you dream, the further you get."

UNIQUE TECHNIQUE

The American swimmer used his dolphin kick to travel as far as possible underwater at the start of races and after turns, giving him a considerable advantage over his opponents.

36

Michael Phelps set 36 world records in his career: 29 individual records and 7 relay records.

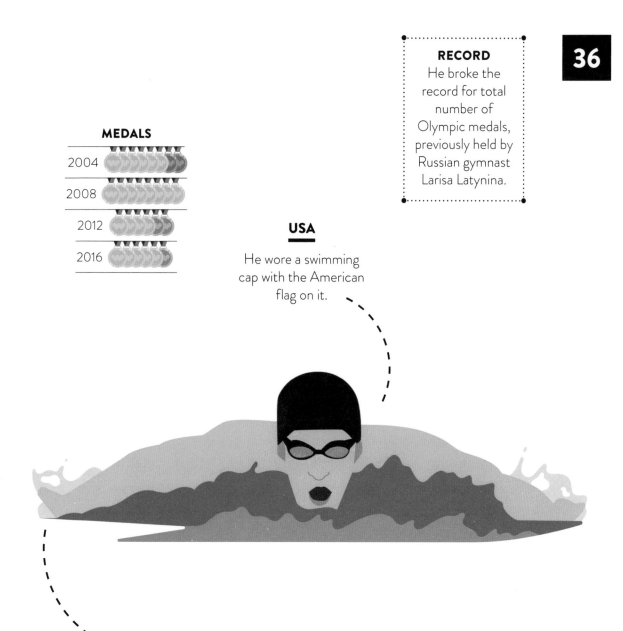

MEDALS

2004

2008

2012

2016

RECORD
He broke the record for total number of Olympic medals, previously held by Russian gymnast Larisa Latynina.

USA
He wore a swimming cap with the American flag on it.

FLIPPERS
Michael Phelps wears size 14 shoes, so his big feet generated a lot of power in the water.

PROPELLERS
He has long arms and a very efficient stroke.

Flying fish

Usain Bolt

BIOGRAPHY

Aug 1986

Jamaican

Athletics

100m, 200m, 4x100m

Main rival: Justin Gatlin (American) and Johan Blake (Jamaican)

Between winning his first major titles in **2008** and retiring in 2017, the Jamaican sprinter established himself as a true legend of the sport. He burst onto the world stage at the Beijing Olympics in 2008, winning triple gold in the 100m, 200m, and 4x100m relay. He repeated this incredible achievement twice, in London and Rio, becoming the only athlete to win those titles at three consecutive Olympics.

ONE DOWN

After winning his triple triple, he equaled Carl Lewis and Paavo Nurmi with a total of nine Olympic titles. But in 2017, the International Olympic Committee stripped him of one medal, as his Jamaican relay teammate Nesta Carter was found guilty of doping.

INCREDIBLE SPEED

When the Jamaican set the 200m world record of 19.19 seconds, he was running at 23.31mph. He went even faster for the 100m record of 9.58 seconds, reaching a speed of 23.35mph.

AFTERWARDS

He tried to follow his childhood dream of becoming a professional soccer player, but although he was good enough to train with a few clubs, he didn't sign with any long term.

After the Rio Olympics, Usain Bolt said, "I hope I've set the bar high enough so that no one can do it again."

37

RECORD

He still holds three world records: 100m in 9.58s (2009), 200m in 19.19s (2009), and 4x100m in 36.84s (2012).

DIFFERENT SCALE

Although recent sprint champions had been shorter and more muscular, he was slimmer and taller (6'5").

CELEBRATIONS

After every win, he did his signature victory pose.

MEDALS

2008
2012
2016

LONG STRIDE

Bolt took on average 41 strides in the 100m, fewer compared to the 44 average steps of his opponents.

Lightning bolt

Teddy Riner

BIOGRAPHY

Apr 1989

French

Judo

Heavyweight

Main rival:
Daiki Kamikawa
(Japanese)

Incredibly agile and quick for a heavyweight, this French judoka has reigned supreme over the tatami mats since 2010. He's won ten world titles since 2007 and also left his mark on the Olympics, winning gold in London and Rio and bronze in Beijing. Now Teddy Riner is setting his sights on a gold medal in Tokyo. If he succeeds, he will be without doubt the greatest judoka of all time.

THE EVENT

Judo made its first appearance at the Tokyo Olympics in 1964, with only men competing. Women had to wait until the Barcelona Games in 1992.

IN GOOD COMPANY

Following in the footsteps of sprinter Marie-José Pérec in Atlanta in 1996 and judoka David Douillet in Sydney in 2000, he was the French flagbearer in Rio, where he won gold.

PRECOCIOUS

In 2007, at just 18, Teddy Riner made his debut on the world stage, beating the Japanese Olympic champion Kosei Inoue, and becoming the youngest ever world champion.

"I don't want to give my opponents anything."

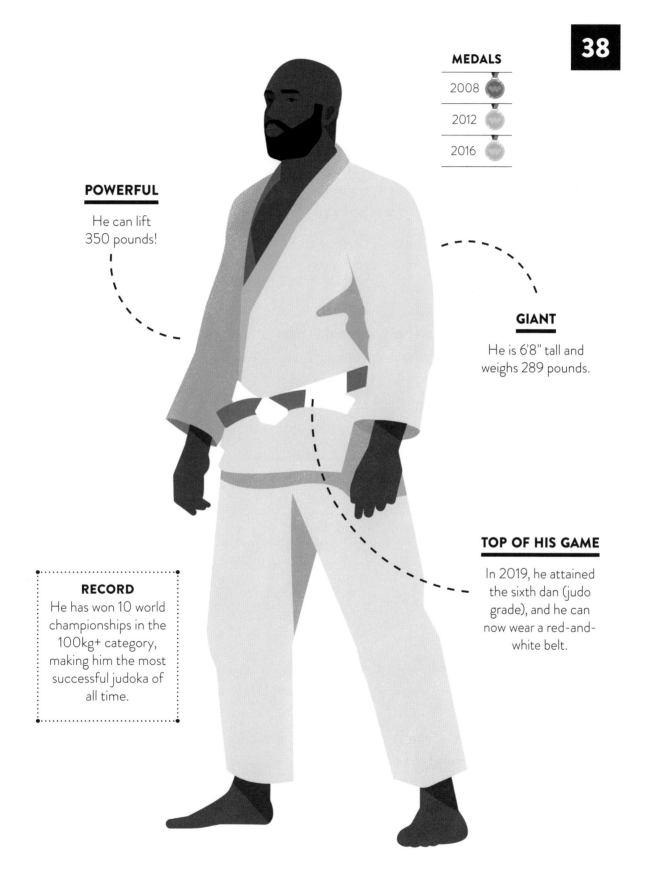

38

MEDALS

2008	
2012	
2016	

POWERFUL

He can lift 350 pounds!

GIANT

He is 6'8" tall and weighs 289 pounds.

RECORD

He has won 10 world championships in the 100kg+ category, making him the most successful judoka of all time.

TOP OF HIS GAME

In 2019, he attained the sixth dan (judo grade), and he can now wear a red-and-white belt.

Teddy bear

Ellie Simmonds

BIOGRAPHY

Nov 1994

British

Swimming

50m, 100m, 200m, 400m freestyle

Main rival: Mirjam de Koning (Dutch)

This popular swimmer is well known in the UK for both her sporting prowess and her charming personality. At just 4 feet tall, Ellie Simmonds is a world champ. She was the youngest British athlete at the 2008 Paralympic Games in Beijing. She competed in five events and took home two gold medals, in the 100m and 400m freestyle. In the 400m, she smashed her own world record, beating it by more than seven seconds! The hero of the pools won gold again at the London and Rio Paralympics.

DETERMINED

Although she's very friendly out of the pool, Ellie Simmonds has a fierce competitive spirit. In her own words, "when we're in the pool, it's war."

AFTERWARDS

After the London Olympics, the Royal Mail issued two postage stamps with her picture on them.

"I'm just a normal person, but a bit smaller than everyone else."

HONEST

As well as her tenacity and will to win, Ellie Simmonds's fans love her honesty and warmth. After winning her first title in the 100m in Beijing, she burst into tears in her first TV interview, happy but exhausted.

39

MEDALS

2008

2012

2016

RECORD
She has beaten 4 para swimming world records.

RECOGNIZABLE
She often wears a swimming cap with her name and the British flag on it.

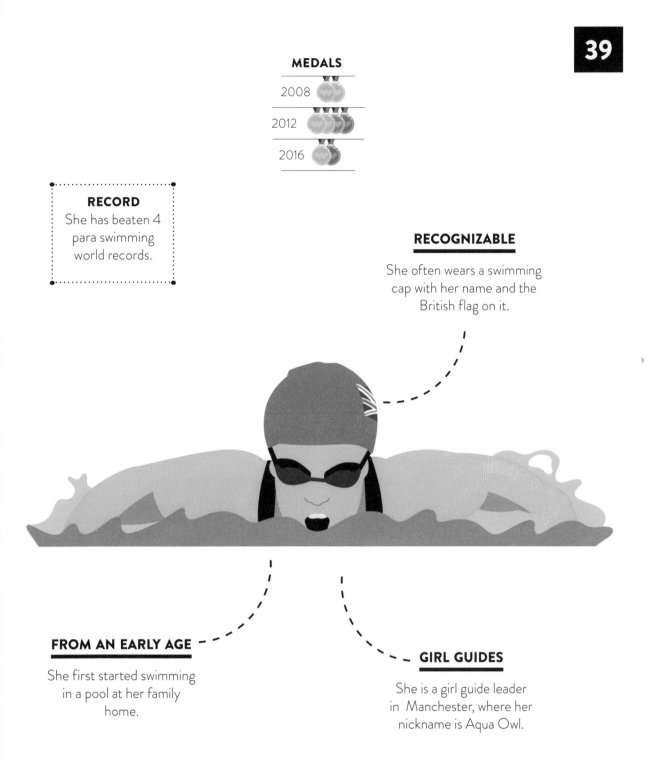

FROM AN EARLY AGE
She first started swimming in a pool at her family home.

GIRL GUIDES
She is a girl guide leader in Manchester, where her nickname is Aqua Owl.

Aqua owl

Simone Biles

BIOGRAPHY

March 1997

American

Artistic gymnastics

General competition, floor, vault, beam

Main rival:
Aly Raisman (American)

This young American gymnast burst onto the scene in 2016 at the Rio Olympics and became one of its biggest breakout stars. Within the space of a few days, she won four gold medals, in the team event and the individual floor, vault, and all-around competitions. This young firecracker from Columbus also finished third in the beam. At only 19 years old, she took her first Olympics by storm and her sporting future burns bright!

CHILD PRODIGY

Simone started practicing gymnastics at age 6. She was amazed when she saw older children in the gym team and knew she had to do it too.

AFTERWARDS

After her incredible victories in 2016, she was the first American gymnast to be chosen as the country's flagbearer at the closing ceremony.

> "I'm not the next Usain Bolt or Michael Phelps. I'm the first Simone Biles."

BREAKING NEW GROUND

In 2013, she was the first gymnast to perform a double layout with a half-twist out in competition. The move is now called "the Biles."

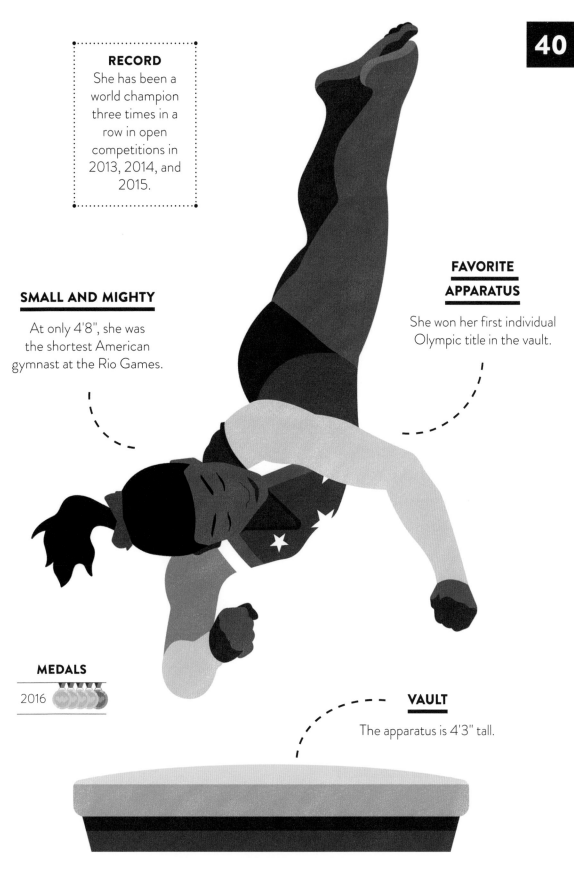

40

RECORD
She has been a world champion three times in a row in open competitions in 2013, 2014, and 2015.

FAVORITE APPARATUS
She won her first individual Olympic title in the vault.

SMALL AND MIGHTY
At only 4'8", she was the shortest American gymnast at the Rio Games.

MEDALS
2016

VAULT
The apparatus is 4'3" tall.

Tumbling queen

Chronology

1896
The first modern Olympic Games
241 male athletes participate in these Games, held in Athens—including 169 Greeks! The others come from 13 European countries as well as Chile, Australia, and the USA.

Greek Spyridon Louis was the first winner of the marathon.

1904
Medalists at the St. Louis Games
For the first time, gold, silver, and bronze medals are awarded, respectively, to the competitors who come first, second, and third in each event.

1928
Amsterdam Games: women on the track
Women are finally allowed to participate in track and field events. An Olympic flame is lit in the main stadium for the first time.

Mildred Didrikson was the star of the 1932 Games.

1948
London: the Olympics on TV
12 years after the Berlin Games and 3 years after the end of World War II, the UK's capital welcomes athletes from all over the world. For the first time, events are broadcast in color.

Fanny Blankers-Koen wins 4 gold medals in athletics.

1972
Hostage crisis at the Munich Games
11 members of the Israeli team are assassinated by the Black September terrorist organization. One West German police officer is killed, along with five of the eight terrorists.

Mark Spitz outclasses all competitors in swimming.

1976
Montreal Games: mascot mania
After Waldi the dachshund, the first official mascot in 1972, Amik the beaver is the star of the Canadian Games. Each Games since have had one or more mascots.

Queen of Gymnastics, Nadia Comăneci, achieves a perfect score of 10.

1920
Antwerp Games: the first oath
Belgian Olympian Victor Boin recited the athletes' oath: "In the name of all competitors, I promise that we shall take part in these Olympic Games, respecting and abiding by the rules that govern them, in the true spirit of sportsmanship, for the glory of sport and the honor of our teams."

The Olympic flame is lit in Olympia, Greece.

1924
The first Winter Olympic Games
Chamonix hosts competitions in bobsled, curling, ice hockey, speed skating, figure skating, cross-country skiing, ski-jumping, Nordic combined skiing, and military patrol (similar to the modern biathlon).

Madge Syers was figure skating champion at the 1908 Summer Olympics.

1952
Helsinki and the Cold War Games
Germany and Japan return to the competition and the Soviet Union participates for the first time. The Olympic Village is divided in two, with athletes from Western countries on one side and Eastern Bloc countries on the other.

Czechoslovakian Emil Zátopek dominates the long-distance races.

1960
Rome: the first Paralympic Games
A week after the Olympics, Rome hosts 400 athletes from 23 countries. 8 sports are planned, including wheelchair basketball and billiards.

Trischa Zorn is the the most successful Paralympian in history.

1992
Barcelona: the complete Games
All countries participate. In 1976, 22 African countries boycotted the games. In 1980, the USA and its allies sat out. In 1984, it was the USRR, and in 1988, 7 countries did not participate.

Steve Redgrave wins his third gold medal in as many Games.

2020
The Tokyo Games
Japan's capital is host city for the second time. Athens (1896, 2004), Paris (1900, 1924, and 2024), London (1908, 1948, and 2012), and Los Angeles (1932, 1984, and 2028) have also hosted multiple times.

TOKYO 2020

Brimming with creative inspiration, how-to projects, and useful information to enrich your everyday life, Quarto Knows is a favorite destination for those pursuing their interests and passions. Visit our site and dig deeper with our books into your area of interest: Quarto Creates, Quarto Cooks, Quarto Homes, Quarto Lives, Quarto Drives, Quarto Explores, Quarto Gifts, or Quarto Kids.

Inspiring | Educating | Creating | Entertaining

Amazing Athletes © 2020 Quarto Publishing plc.

First Published in 2020 in French by Gallimard Jeunesse, France.
First Published in 2020 in English by Wide Eyed Editions, an imprint of The Quarto Group,400 First Avenue North, Suite 400, Minneapolis, MN 55401, USA.
T (612) 344-8100 F (612) 344-8692 **www.QuartoKnows.com**

A catalog record for this book is available from the British Library.

ISBN 978-0-71125-254-7

The illustrations were created digitally
Set in Brandon Grotesque and Gotham Rounded

Translated by Bethany Wright
Edited by Lucy Brownridge
Designed by Myrto Dimitrakoulia
Production by Dawn Cameron

Manufactured in Guangdong, China CC012020
9 8 7 6 5 4 3 2 1

Collect the rest in the series!

Soccer Stars
978-1-78603-142-6

Greek Gods & Heroes
978-1-78603-143-3

Music Legends
978-1-78603-145-7

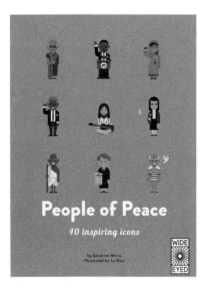

People of Peace
978-1-78603-144-0

People of Peace
978-1-78603-144-0

Super Scientists
978-1-78603-474-8